Broken

A FRONTLINE COUNSELOR'S GUIDE
FOR HEALING

Courtnay Aycock, MA

TRILOGY CHRISTIAN PUBLISHERS
TUSTIN,

Trilogy Christian Publishers A Wholly Owned Subsidiary of Trinity Broadcasting Network

2442 Michelle Drive Tustin, CA 92780

Broken: A Frontline Counselor's Guide for Healing

Cover design by Jeff Summers

For information about special discounts for bulk purchases, please contact Trilogy Christian Publishing.

Manufactured in the United States of America

10 9 8 7 6 5 4 3 2 1

Library of Congress Cataloging-in-Publication Data is available.

ISBN: 978-1-63769-870-9

E-ISBN: 978-1-63769-871-6

Contents

David, we have dedicated our lives to Christ and to each other, so it feels natural that I would dedicate this book to you. You have loved me at my best, and you have loved me when I was so broken that I had nothing left to give. Thank you for helping make this book possible and believing in me when it felt like things were impossible. Thank you for teaching me to dream. We need at least fifty more years together, and we haven't even started counting yet...

Acknowledgements

It is difficult to thank all of the people that have helped me form the thoughts and words that have made this book possible. I have to first and always thank Jesus because He is who I run to for my healing and for the healing of every person that shares their pain with me.

David, you are my best friend, biggest supporter, and the one that shows me the love of Jesus every single day. I love you. Thank you for the four million hours of listening to me read this book, convincing me that someone might want to publish it, and reminding me to be brave.

Jessica and Tyler, I am so blessed that I am your momma. Although God could not have given me two children that are any more different from each other, He has used you both to shape me and make me into the woman that I am today.

Bethany, you are so many things to me that I would run out of paper listing them. You are my Ruth: so precious, sacrificial, and wise. This book would not have happened without all of your help. I love you and am so thankful for you.

Melissa, this book would not have started without your insight, encouragement, and wisdom. Thank you for being a warrior and a friend.

Anne, not many friends would stay up until 2 a.m. in a mountain cabin or give up time from your busy schedule to be my editor, thought processor, and dear friend, all at the same time. You are a treasure beyond words.

Dad, I am thankful for your wisdom and your sense of humor that I may have inherited. I am thankful that you are always a phone call away. I would not be who I am today without you and Mary.

Heather, you are stronger than you ever thought you were. I am thankful that we could find laughter in a chemo room. Ah, sisters. Thank you for letting me share and be in your story.

To my clients, no one will ever know who you are, but your stories have changed me, and now they can help others. I continue to pray for your healing.

To our friends that God made family, our "framily": Chris, Aletia, Dean, Anne, Darren, Wava, Bethany, Rebecca, Melissa, Brad, Billy, and Jean; you are our circle, our people that we depend on. We prayed for people like you to come into our lives. Thank you from the bottom of our hearts. You helped make this possible by praying for us, challenging us, and loving us.

To Brad, Jody, and all of those at Trilogy Christian Publishing, thank you for believing in me. It is an honor to work with such incredible people on a wild adventure like this.

"God uses broken things. It takes broken soil to produce a crop, broken clouds to give rain, broken grain to give bread, broken bread to give strength. It is the broken alabaster box that gives forth perfume."

—Vance Havner

Preface

I tried to write a book about anything else. Birds, planes, guitars, flutes; pick a topic, I tried it. I actually have four other books started. You may ask yourself why would a sane person do such an insane thing. Because I really felt in my heart that God was telling me to write a book. So, I would write. I wrote books and would actually start to like parts of them, but then I would feel like "I am writing this out of obedience, but I would never actually read this book." So, I would start another book. I even told my Board of Directors at the Ministry about my call to write a book so they would hold me accountable. And they did. And I kept writing for many years.

One day, I was having breakfast with one of my dear friends. She asked how my book was going. I told her about all my frustration. In all of her kind wisdom, she said, "Why don't you write a book about your life and how you help people? That's what people really need to hear." As we talked through my life, I felt something deep inside of me that I had never felt. I came home that day and wrote the first two chapters of this book and felt something in my soul. I knew this was the book. I rarely read books or watch teachers that have had perfect lives. My life has been held together by thin threads of bad decisions and thick ropes of grace for so long. If their lives were too perfect, I feel a little too undone. So when God called me to ministry, I felt humbled, honored, and unworthy, all at the same time. Trust me, I understand broken and God putting you back together in a million different ways.

When I was in high school, there was only one university I wanted to attend, Liberty. When the colleges visited our school one day, I got information from one college, that was it. People even signed it in my yearbook, "Have fun at Liberty!", "See you at Liberty!" My plans and my future felt secure until I found out I was pregnant with my daughter. I traded textbooks for diapers and two jobs. She may have been unplanned, but she was not unwanted.

Fast forward to 2012, and my husband, David, my daughter Jessica, who is very pregnant with our grandson Parker, and I are headed to Liberty University. I am finally going, and I am graduating, with my Master's degree, as a graduate with the highest distinction. As we went to register, they handed me a medal to wear around my neck for being in the top 1 percent of my class, and I wept; David had to hold me up while I was weeping. See, it hit me that God has never forgotten me and my dreams and those yearbooks or textbooks from high school. He honored what I did not feel I deserved. He saw all the years of sacrifice and brokenness, and I felt like in that moment at the Rotunda in Liberty University, I got a medal at the end. There has never been a happier graduate than the woman who stood on that campus next to her daughter, pregnant with her grandson, holding her degree. I was sure I even heard the heavens applaud.

The reason I share that story with you in the preface of this book is I want you to have a little glimpse of who wrote it. I have walked out brokenness many times. I have walked out the steps I wrote about. I have not found healing in a day or through some quick fix. It has been hard work, but healing is worth it. How much time and energy are you spending on maintaining being broken? Why not spend that same time taking steps towards healing? It is time to change your identity, my friend. Broken doesn't have to be who you are.

This book, like my life, has only been possible by God's providential grace. Thank you for taking the time to read it.

The Shortest
Longest Chapter
of My Life

Positive. That was what she said, but my ears could not process the word that would make it reach the deep recesses of my brain. "Can you please run it again?" The sweet older lady with the kind eyes looked at me with a confused but compassionate nod. She reemerged, sat down, and explained to me that the likelihood that two pregnancy tests being positive and wrong was highly unlikely. I looked around the cramped little room, stacked to the ceiling with diapers, containers of donated clothing, cribs, swings, and other baby needs, and I couldn't think or speak or cry. Yes, Courtnay has officially left the building. The sweet lady began the talk, "Do you have a support system in place? What will your parents think? Do you have insurance? Do you plan on keeping the baby? How do you feel about abortion? We can help you."

When I think back to that day over thirty years ago, the more she asked, the smaller that room became. Decades later, that conversation would shape how I counseled and helped other women in my shoes, as well as how I advised others in hard and broken situations.

Now, back to my sixteen-year-old self. My thoughts were, *My mother is struggling to raise me, my support system is my youth group and Jesus, I am sixteen years old, I don't know anything about insurance* (it seemed like a weird question, but I'm sure it made sense to an adult mind), *I don't have any idea; five minutes ago I didn't know there even was a baby (random thought—why do you have things stacked to the ceiling?), and I know I will not have an abortion.*

Looking back, I didn't realize how young I was. I thought I knew so much, and I truly was mature for my age, but I was not an adult by any stretch of the imagination. When we see a teenage mom or someone else that we judge and assume we know their past, their present, and their future, we need to remember that only God does. He knows it all. I thought that the plans I had for my future were forever gone. They were delayed, and they were changed as God changed me.

It has been over thirty-two years since I gave birth to my daughter. Through the amazing grace of God, I have shattered so many statistics that the world said I never would. Through every single failure, hardship, and heartbreak, God was building a ministry and making a new me. It's been a beautiful mess, and I pray it helps to encourage you and get you on the path to healing. I pray that this book gives you the steps that you need to find your way out of the darkness. I am quite familiar with the difficulty of dark, hard places. I pray that whoever reads this book finds hope in knowing that there is a God in heaven that specializes in repairing broken things. This may be the first step on your path to finding healing and having your pieces put back together again.

How do you find hope in the hopelessness you may feel? How do you take a first step towards the light when you feel you are surrounded by darkness?

First, address your spiritual life. Have you talked to your Heavenly Father about the hopelessness that you feel? The Great Physician really needs to hear from you in prayer. Have you searched the scriptures to find words of hope to stand on?

Second, get a physical. That may sound like I have taken a wrong turn here, but many health conditions can make the darkness we face even darker. And please be honest with your physician about everything that you are feeling.

And third, address what is making you feel hopeless. Have you actually thought about what is making you feel sad, stuck, or depressed? Have you found a trusted friend, a pastor, or counselor that can help you with what you are going through? We were not meant to go through life alone. Loneliness breeds hopelessness.

When I have walked through the hardest parts of my life, I never walked alone. I always had Jesus and a few people I could trust to help me through. I had to look for them, though. I had to position myself in places where Godly people would be. When we are broken, we need help to be healed. Psalm 147:3 (NIV) promises us, "He heals the brokenhearted and binds up their wounds." I can promise you this, God is faithful to all of His promises and will heal you. Stand upon His promises, and let's begin putting the broken pieces back together again.

Survival, Sanity, and Other Endangered Species

Women have this incredible ability to be sensitive and fragile and yet made out of impenetrable titanium, all at the same time. This loving, unexplainable strength proves that we are created in the image of God. He is tender in His mercies towards us, and yet we see His power and might in the roaring of the seas and the wonder and beauty of His creation. We, as women, show these incredible, unique qualities of God in our ability to give birth or to raise children. I am always in awe at the strength of a woman and her sacrificial love that is displayed in the beautiful exchange of adoption. A birth mother that loves her baby enough to give that precious child into the arms of another mama is such a beautiful exchange that I believe even the angels weep.

You see another incredible display of the glorious strength of a woman when she is caring for a dying loved one. Watching a woman stay by a loved one's side until their very last breath on earth is an incredible thing of strength and courage. Two of my dearest friends on this planet have recently held their mothers' hands and loved and cared for their every need until they saw Jesus face to face. They both told me a slight variation of the same theme, "It was such an honor to be there until the end. There is nowhere else I can imagine being." This is incredible, beautiful God-like love with strength drenched in servanthood.

Have you seen and mustered raw fortitude and grace when a health crisis comes knocking on *your* front door? Has the knock come for you or a loved one? Your world and what you thought about the future can vanish right in front of you like the sun on a rainy day. Yet, somehow, we as women have this ability to fight the devil himself with Holy Spirit fire in our bones while making a lemon pound cake with our hands for someone else in need at the exact same time. That is just what we do. We are women. *Imago Dei*, Latin for "created in the image of God." In these and a million other moments of time, we are given the opportunities to show the world that we are, indeed, image-bearers for Him.

How is this possible? How does this happen in everyday life, in a million different ways? I have been honored and blessed to listen to thousands of hours of ladies' stories, as well as living out my own. If I didn't know better, I would think we could not survive the things that we do. As a pastoral counselor, I have walked with women at their lowest, most broken moments. There are no words to describe what that experience has been like for me.

You may have heard of the term burnout. Many of you may be thinking, "Courtnay, I bought the 'burnout' T-shirt, and it immediately burst into flames." If you have not heard the phrase burnout or have heard it but are not completely sure what it means, burnout is when we wear ourselves out by doing the same things over and over until we are absolutely wiped out. I have found that we as women can suffer from this because we tend to be caregivers of those around us, compounded by the fact that we are not so great at taking care of ourselves.

Counselors of all kinds have ridiculously high burnout rates. We could be awesome Olympic athletes, except that we are all so tired that during training sessions, we would be sleeping in our cars after eating bags of chocolate, crying hysterically, still in our pajama pants. We cannot take any more pressure from people, and it's not a pretty picture. Counseling is hard work. If I am completely honest with you, I have personally coped with the stresses of counseling for many years through a few different methods. They have been tightly held secrets up until now, so, please, don't tell anybody.

I pray. I have prayed constantly, like while my clients are talking, inside of my head. The pain that women have somehow survived is so insurmountable that I have no words, no thoughts, so I listen, and I pray constantly. God gives me the grace and the words to give comfort. God has always, one hundred percent of the time, given me what I needed for the woman in front of me. You want to know why? Because they are so precious to Him that they just needed someone to show up for them. I want to provide His comfort. I desperately want to be a conduit of His grace and love and, when we pray, we get to be just that.

I cry. I remember when I first got out of school telling myself, *You can't cry harder than the client; you cannot cry harder than the client.* So, I asked the Lord to help me have the strength to be the person filled with compassion but to be professional enough to be strong. So, I listened, and I had tissues and a comfortable room and tender words of mercy. I have prayed at the conclusion of counseling with every client, with their permission, but one, because she declined. When the day is done, and my notes are written, and everything is locked up, I get in my car, and I weep. I weep all the way home. I weep for every woman whose loved one died. I weep for every broken vow, every diagnosis, every mental illness. I weep for every woman that feels unloved by her husband and her children. I weep for the financial stresses and the sexual abuse that cannot be undone but just leaves deep scars that are unseen to those around her. I fill the napkins in my car door, the ones I shoved in there from whatever drive-thru I went through last, with the pain that those women entrusted to me. I sit in my car, in my driveway, and I thank God that every single one of those women trusted me. It is an honor that I am constantly in awe of. I will never share their stories. Well, sort of. Normally in my day, this is when my husband, David, hears that I am home. After all these years, he knows my routine; he opens the door, smiles at me to let me know he is here and the door is unlocked, but he knows I am not done with my day. I still have to finish up. I used to not do this last part, and I was burning out faster than an ember in a white-hot fire. My SUV becomes my own little chapel, and I give all of these precious women to Jesus. I mentally go through each precious woman, by name, in the privacy of my car, and I tell the Lord that only He can save and only He can heal. They may be my clients, but they are His children. I mentally imagine setting each of them at the foot of the cross and the healing, perfect blood of Christ covering their overwhelming situations. I feel ten tons lighter. I feel like I have made a difference in each of their eternities.

Then, I get out of my car (bag full of napkins from drive-thru in hand), and I am ready to see my man, and I make myself laugh. Okay, listen, I told you these are the secrets to my sanity. Don't start judging me now. Proverbs 17:22 (NIV) says, "A cheerful heart is good medicine, but a crushed spirit dries up the bones." Let me put some context around this. When you are going through, coming through, or heading out of hard, hard times, you need some times of joy. You probably won't find joy about the thing that is awful. I have never come home from a really hard day of counseling and found anything funny or joy-filled about that. But, to keep my sanity, I come home to my precious husband, and we watch silly shows on TV or stupid videos online, or he tells me jokes until I am laughing hysterically. A cheerful heart is good medicine. I need the medicine to survive the hard. I think one of a million gifts of being a Christian woman is that we can survive the hard by finding the joy of Jesus. If I didn't have eternal hope, I wouldn't be able to laugh at anything at the end of a hard day. I wouldn't be able to find any joy in the midst of so many things that should have destroyed me, and yet joy pokes through my life like a weed in the crack of a sidewalk daily. It's God's mercies if you are open to look for them, and it will keep you sane.

Why do I share these three things with you? Because you are warriors, and you have more strength than you know. But you may be tired and weary and need some direction. Read your Bible always. What I do as a counselor can help you get through your hard everyday life.

Pray. Talk to God in your head as you go throughout your day. Talk to Him anytime that you can and anytime that you will. God longs to hear from you and loves you. There is no detail of your life you can't talk to Him about.

Cry. I think we are afraid to cry because we are afraid we won't stop. We are afraid we will be perceived as weak. Maybe it would be healing. Maybe you have gone through things that should be wept over. Maybe you never cry over the awful, and running from your pain is leaving you stuck when you are ready to move on. Tears are not the enemy. Jesus Himself wept. It can be so healing and cleansing.

Laugh. We look around at the world today and may struggle to find much to be happy about. It may feel wrong, and yet, there are physical, mental, and spiritual benefits to laughter. Laughter can help you feel joy and hope again. Watch some old, old sitcoms, play a board game, dance to old music, find your happy.

You are an amazing woman of God. You will get through this. Pray, cry, and I am telling you, dear sister, you will, indeed, laugh again.

When the Earth Stands Still

Boom. No warning, no alarms sounded. No one called the police. I looked around, and no one else even looked surprised or shaken up at all. I could barely hear. I could not even remember where I parked my car. And yet, I just could not understand how my entire world could be so turned upside down and everyone else on the planet would be so, dare I say, fine?

I have learned every day since that this happens to us all and has happened to me unfortunately many times in the course of my life. Traumatic events leave a mark, a scar, a void that changes you. This particular day, my son was diagnosed with type 1 diabetes, a very uncommon type. Type 1 diabetes is nothing like type 2 diabetes. Type 1 makes up less than 10 percent of all diabetics, and I knew very little about either one. See, Tyler had no symptoms; we had gone to visit his doctor for a healthy check-up the day before kindergarten began. My precious pediatrician even told me, "I don't know how to tell you this, but he has type 1 diabetes. You won't remember anything else I say, go home, and pack a bag for the hospital. Your life will never be the same." That sentence was the last words I could remember from his visit, and I still remember them twenty years later. Our lives were never the same. I have never slept the same, planned the same, or shopped the same. We also have an incredibly remarkable, resilient son, and yet that day changed his life forever. Tyler was only five years old, one of the youngest kids to be diagnosed by his pediatrician at that time. When he started to go through middle and high school, more kids were being diagnosed. He became the kid who had it the longest, so he could offer hope and encouragement and be the newly diagnosed kid's friend. I would get messages and phone calls from other grateful mommas, saying Tyler was the one to help their child feel more normal or not be bullied. I was the mom that had taken care of insurance companies (okay, fought with insurance companies), balanced insulin regimens, and managed food logs, so I could help with all the overwhelming stuff, plus the trauma of *that day*. That awful day when you are being changed, but you don't know it yet. You don't know how big what you just heard is, but you are terrified all the same. I could be there for those parents because I really understood that. Broken can minister to broken; Psalm 42:7 (NIV) says, "Deep calls unto deep."

When I worked in a residential treatment center for addiction, I would get asked on a regular basis, "What are you in recovery from?" There was an understanding from some of the residents that if you weren't in recovery from something, then they didn't feel you had an understanding about their pain and struggles of addiction. I think a lot of us that have gone through trauma or hurt are in need of someone who has gone through similar hurts to relate to. There is something incredibly comforting about talking to someone who has gone through the same thing as you because they know the lingo, the similar hurts, fears, and feelings.

Cancer. That word is scary and hard. That word has a completely different meaning when you are on the receiving end of the phone call from the doctor's office. In 2020, we had four people close to us get that call that no one wants. My sister was one of them, and I was blessed to be able to go with her to her appointments and chemotherapy. Her treatment plan was grueling. After months of chemotherapy, she had a double mastectomy, then six weeks of radiation, and a hysterectomy. After all the surgery, treatments, procedures, fear, anxiety, and emotions, she could not handle the "C" word anymore. We all decided to call it a whole bunch of other words; trauma does a lot of damage that must be dealt with. It can change the heart and mind if left alone and untreated. And yet, she now has the capability to help other survivors in a unique and powerful way. Deep calls unto deep.

Suicide. I think of the precious ladies I have counseled who have lost loved ones to suicide. That is a trauma that is so uniquely painful. It leaves a lot of questions that will not be answered on this side of heaven. How in this world do we survive it? There are insensitive people that say and do the most unbelievable things because they do not understand that some wounds never quite heal. They are held together by divine power that gets you through another day, one day at a time. And yet, these powerful, broken women can minister to other broken women in a way that no one else quite can.

Deep calls unto deep. Pain, trauma, and brokenness are common to all people. I have experienced more than my fair share, and I am sure I have inflicted it upon others as well. We are all human. I think about my time counseling with different women and all the different stories I have been trusted to hear. I think about sitting down with my girlfriends, where an hour melts into six because you start talking and you just relate to each other's pain, and time loses all relativity. We may not have all gone through the same pain and trauma, but there are some commonalities that we all can relate to. If we can agree that that can be true, then there are things we can do to find some help and healing.

Those of us that have experienced trauma tend to have ways that we have learned to hide it and cope to some degree. We can function in day-to-day life. I like to think of our trauma as our own trauma tent. We put all of our "trauma baggage" inside of the tent. Some of us have big tents, and some have small tents. What is interesting about the people I see and for myself is that the baggage inside of my tent doesn't come out every single day. I have trauma related to many things, but let's use the medical office with my son for an example. Whenever I had to take him back to the doctor, my tent, with all of its baggage, showed up with anxiety and so much fear. The objects that would trigger me: seeing the medical office again, the smell of the cleaner, the tiles on the floor, and the artwork on the wall. As soon as I walked into the office, my baggage and my tent formed the perfect jacked-up campground. I was so afraid that another bombshell would be dropped in my lap. *I mean, the last time I walked into this place, things were fine, and then, "our lives will never be the same" happened. What could happen today?* Does anyone else ever feel that way when they have to visit a place, physically or emotionally, that has been traumatic, but they still have to go there? Here is how I broke free from my cycle. I still use these tools, and many others have found hope as well.

One of the most powerful tools that I use for myself and with my clients is this simple and easy-to-remember phrase: *this* is not *that*. I keep reminding my brain that *this* experience is not *that* experience. Our minds tend to tie smells, sights, sounds, and emotions to past and painful experiences—the more traumatic, the stronger the tie. The good news is that brains can be renewed and retaught with time and practice. For me, I had to remind myself that *this* visit with my son is not *that* visit. *This* is a new day; *that* day is gone. I have a brand new day here; that experience is over. The old has passed away; the new has come. *This* _____ is not *that* _____. Fill in the blanks with whatever your area of trauma is.

If you are experiencing an area of trauma that is repeating, in other words, you are having to say this over and over because the exact same event continues to happen to you, please get help. If you are in an abusive relationship or situation where trauma continues to repeat itself, go to the police, to the closest emergency room, or call 911. Tell a coworker or your pastor, but you must make the trauma stop before further damage happens to you. You must also know that kind of trauma is not God's plan for you. Sometimes in life, we are hit with trauma like a lightning bolt, and the Lord wants to heal us from the aftershocks and pain that results. Ongoing trauma at the hands of another needs to end now.

The second tool we should remember is that we always need the Word of God to break free from painful experiences and to find healing. I personally used this verse: "For God has not given us a spirit of fear, but of power and of love and of a sound mind" (2 Timothy 1:7, NIV). No matter what type of trauma you have experienced, this is a powerful verse that continues to give me strength and courage. I memorized this verse and told myself this over and over. As God's daughter, I am not meant to live under a *spirit* of fear. I have power and a sound mind.

Whenever I went to unpack my trauma tent in an anxiety or fear-filled place, I would do these two things, and my tent got pretty small and manageable.

There can be a redemptive side to our trauma tent. In God's hands, He can use anything. We can take our trauma tent to someone else's trauma tent and camp out, just for a little while. It's not a competition of who's trauma is more or less awful; it's a tent of empathy and support so we can understand their pain. We can unpack for a while and tend to their brokenness in the same way we know Christ shows up at our place of pain. We can share our anxiety, fear, and places where we felt really low. Then we share how we survived. We share how we began to expose our pain before the Lord. We allowed Him to uncover the dark recesses and fear-filled places that our trauma tents hid and covered. We allowed Him to begin to work on the rough and rugged canvas that we have kept all of our baggage hidden in for so long. We began to realize that our tent was a place where the enemy tried to destroy us, but instead, God made something incredible. Do we come out of trauma the same? Well...

There is an amazing thing about trauma tents. We use them to hide in and store all of our wounded, broken, ugly baggage that we don't know what to do with. We just want it to go away. But guess what? Our Father is a Master Tailor; did you know that? He takes hard, unpliable canvas and, when we let go of it and place it into His hands, He starts to use a pattern that was custom made just for you. He forms and fashions it to fit every place that was wounded and broken. The tent that used to hide you becomes a gown of beauty that radiates the glory of the Savior that carried you through. What was meant to destroy you will save someone else. In their saving, you will find more healing because your testimony matters. So please, put on that gown that was made from your broken pieces; after all, it's a one-of-a-kind masterpiece, custom made just for you. Go and shine His glory. Only He can make something so spectacular from something so traumatic. Don't waste all that beautiful; the angels in heaven are envious of you.

I delight greatly in the Lord; my soul rejoices in my God. For he has clothed me with garments of salvation and arrayed me in a robe of his righteousness, as a bridegroom adorns his head like a priest, and as a bride adorns herself with her jewels.

Isaiah 61:10 (NIV)

You Better Know Your Place

I am not sure where I was or how young I was the first time I heard this phrase. I can't say it was at home because I was more apt to cry than to rebel. I may have heard it with a friend, or at school, or while watching TV. We had amazing television shows to watch when I was a kid. My sister and I would watch a popular show about a cruise ship, *The Love Boat*[1]. Every time it came on, we had to race to be the first one to get to the set. You had to call it a set back then, not a television. We had never even thought of a flat-screen. The television set was encased in such a huge slab of semi-wood-like material that may have been a twelve-inch screen, but it was so large that half of your living room was television and wood. Today, we would slap a porch on the front and sell them as tiny houses. But back in the day, we coated them in lemon-scented chemicals to make them shine and luster. Oh my, the good old days.

We would race to get to the set because we had a game we played. We always got to choose what character we were in that episode. Whatever the characters did, we got to do. If they laughed, we laughed; they cried, we cried. I mean, we were that character for the *entire episode*. It was an important role and a seriously big deal. Shows like *The Facts of Life*[2] were full of great girl roles, but *The Love Boat* only had one, and we both wanted it: Julie, the cruise director. Julie was pretty and smart, and her role was who we wanted to be. Whoever got there first won; she was Julie for the whole episode. That meant if we wanted to make fun of the one who lost, we could. Nothing changed our Julie status. The rules were clear and simple. We knew our place.

Well, adolescence and adulthood threw a big old monkey wrench in all of that clear and simpleness. Our relationships became more than one-dimensional. They lasted more than an hour and didn't have a few commercial interruptions so we could go get a snack. They began to bring genuine laughter and memories that were forged into our brains. We started to feel love in different and exciting ways. These relationships started to influence how we view the world and ourselves. We began to have our hearts broken. We began to talk about others, and they began talking about us. We learned that words can destroy lives, shatter dreams, and end friendships that we thought would last forever. We lost pieces of our innocence. We knew we were called to forgive others and ourselves. And over and over again, I just wanted to go back and be Julie.

The complexities of relationship dynamics could be its own book. What I have discovered in my own life and in my own work is that one of the largest stumbling blocks—well, boulders—okay, mountains, to relationships not working is that we want something to be healthy and functional that, simply put, is not. It may have been at one point, or you wanted it to be because it should have been, but it, sadly, is not. It is one of the saddest and hardest realities of my life to admit, but many of my relationships have failed because people wanted me to be something that I could never be, or I wanted them to be something they never were.

I wanted them to love me more, and they couldn't even love themselves. I wanted them to be trustworthy, but I found out they were gossips. I wanted them to be my friends, and they didn't like me. I wanted them to be in my life forever and then discovered they weren't even interested in having lunch together.

I have been dealing with the realities of a new phase of life. When the Lord is changing your season, I have learned that some people remain, and some people were not meant to be a part of the journey. It is so incredibly painful, and yet, I trust the Lord and His goodness in the hard parts of life. Many times this doesn't mean a relationship ends; it means that you have been defining it as something that is not only inaccurate but damaging.

There are people that continue to hurt us and that we excuse because we either have a long history with them, we are accustomed to the dysfunction, they are family, or we are so grace-filled that we continue to make excuses for behavior that is tearing our hearts to shreds. We get so frustrated with them, but I am going to tell you what the Holy Spirit convicted me of, which inspired me to write this to you: *know your place.* If they repeatedly hurt you, love them, pray for them, now more than you ever have, but stop making excuses. You are not as important to them as you think you are. You don't treat valuable things the way you are being treated. This is about being treated with the God-given respect that you deserve if you are doing respectable things. Your place is to guard your heart and stop being someone's emotional punching bag.

I told my husband, David, I was writing this, and he gave me such great insight about how we tend to view people we have relationships with that treat us with such disrespect, and we continue to excuse it. David reminded me, "Do you remember the story of Daniel in the lion's den? The expectation was that the lions would devour Daniel. What about Shadrach, Meshach, and Abednego? They were thrown into the fire and were expected to be burned alive. Lions will be lions. No one told them to go and eat the people thrown into the den. Fires will be fires. No one told the fire to burn hot and consume everything in its path."

People that have a pattern of hurting you don't have to be told what to do because we have told them by our not telling them what to do. Every time they have hurt us with their words, actions, and absence, we have allowed bad behavior to run like a lion and burn like a fire in our lives.

We must speak up and develop healthy boundaries. We must learn to say no when it is appropriate to say so. We must learn to value ourselves as much as God does. We must pray, speak kind words about those that may be hurting us, but stop allowing ourselves to be broken when it is time to be put back together. Sometimes counseling and distance are needed for a time to find true healing. And some relationships sadly never heal.

Woman of God, it's time to guard your heart, put up some boundaries, use your voice, speak up for your needs, fast, and pray. You are a child of God. Know your place.

Anger: Check Your Coat at the Door

Anger. Just the word itself makes me squirm a bit. I am not a person that typically struggles with anger. I struggle with plenty of other things, but anger didn't really make the top ten list. Being around angry people makes me super uncomfortable. Don't get me wrong here; I am not a saint. I have been mad before, but the occasion is rare and typically is after a ridiculously long period of time. I have realized that I am an angry person's worst nightmare. So if you have road rage, I would like to apologize now and ask you to skip ahead a few paragraphs.

When I am uncomfortable in a situation, I tend to cope with humor. Do you know what makes a really angry person a lot angrier? Laughter. Now, I don't mean I have laughed at a loved one or a client who is angry, nor would I ever. I am going to talk about the roots of anger that come out in those relational situations in a moment. Those are real and quite different than the nonsense I am getting ready to waste your time explaining. I am talking about a different, more superficial type of anger here.

One of my favorite wrong reactions that happens to me is bad drivers that do things and then get furious and act like a crazy bird to me. I thankfully do not have road rage, but my reaction to their anger is to laugh hysterically. David thinks this is one of a million eccentricities about me, but I am genuinely amused when you are mad at me because you pulled out four inches in front of me and threw a soft drink out the window and hit my windshield. That seemed like an acceptable response to inappropriate placement of my car within thirty-six inches of your driving space. You should absolutely blow your horn at me in outrage. I am telling you, I am crying with laughter as I go to the car wash to deal with that soft drink situation. There just seems to be bigger problems in the world and, *obviously*, I was wrong. I am officially a weirdo.

Now, let's talk about *real anger*. Anger is an overflowing of negative emotions that means you are *really* dissatisfied. This really strong emotion of dissatisfaction can lead to rage. Rage is the kind of anger that blows up relationships, hurts people's hearts, feels unexplainable, and destroys everything you love if left unchecked. Proverbs 22:24-25 (NIV) even gives us this serious warning: "Do not make friends with a hot-tempered person, do not associate with one easily angered, or you may learn their ways and get yourself ensnared."

This sounds like anger can even be contagious. Have you ever been in an argument with someone who is mad at you? We all tend to go into defense mode, not even hearing the next thing that is being said because we need to make certain we are not torn to shreds. We can fall into that trap so easily, and it is so difficult to be the person that stops the madness and doesn't respond defensively. It goes against our human nature.

So how do we get into so much trouble with anger? We aren't born this way, but anger is an excellent insulator and protector from people around us. It can keep people away from getting too close or asking too many questions.

Anger is really like a heavy winter coat with many layers of hurt-filled experiences underneath it. Some of the experiences are many years old, from past people that have hurt us. Some are past traumas that we have never confessed to a person we know. We have abandonment, self-loathing, old scars, and regrets, all tucked away and balanced underneath that winter coat. Over the years and through many hurts, that coat has become quite heavy and hard to balance, but it hides and protects so much. After all, no one has ever seen me without my angry coat!

That, my friends, is how I view anger. Anger is a "layered condition." I have not gotten really, really angry very many times in my fifty years on planet Earth. And yet, each and every time, when I looked back and started to evaluate my actions and responses, my anger had been building for a long time. Layer upon layer of hurt, frustration, and hopelessness had been building up. Some of those awful layers had been put on me, and some of those layers I put on myself and didn't know what to do with them, so I just covered them all with a coat of anger. But eventually, anger was the explosive device that blew some of that clothing off of me or at least made me aware that I was being buried alive by it.

Anger is protective, just like a winter coat. If I see two people in a room and one is crying, and the other is screaming, I am running to help the one that is crying, the one without the coat. Which one would you run to? Anger keeps you from being vulnerable. Yes, it keeps people away, but it also keeps you alone. Are you tired of being alone? Could you risk being a little less angry and allowing someone safe in? Ephesians 4:31-32 (NIV) teaches us: "Let all bitterness and wrath and anger and clamor and slander be put away from you, along with all malice. Be kind to one another, tender-hearted, forgiving each other, just as God in Christ also has forgiven you."

If Jesus is the standard and He has chosen to forgive me, I can choose to love as He has loved me. Kindness is part of that plan.

I have heard so many people say things like, "Courtnay, I can't help it. I am just an angry person. My mom was angry, her mom was angry, it's how I am made." I get it. We all have a tendency towards things. We all have a leaning, a drive towards things that are destructive. When we have grown up in situations that can be challenging, abusive, or toxic, it is hard, so incredibly hard, to feel like we could ever break free from the only us that we have ever known. But we can. Through the powerful blood of Jesus Christ, tools like Christian counseling, and support groups, we can.

Here are a few things you can do on your own to help you get started:

1. Identify what makes you angry: if you can identify what makes you angry, you may be able to limit your exposure to those triggers or get counseling to create tools when you are exposed to them.

2. Take a time out: decide on the front end how long you need and communicate that to the person you are in conflict with. It's not fair to leave them wondering how long or where you are going while you cool down.

3. Spend time in the Word of God during your time out: seek out devotionals or scriptures that deal with anger and meditate on them.

4. Start to exercise: even a brief walk can help you deal with your anger before you work to resolve it with the person you are in conflict with.

There is this amazing thing about winter coats and all the layers that are worn for years and years underneath them. When we walk with Jesus Christ, we don't have to carry heavy burdens or heavy clothes. We can give Him our heavy emotions, burdensome pain, and destructive anger. This can be the most successful weight loss plan in the entire world. You can lose the weight of your anger and, finally, once and for all, check that coat of anger at the door for the last time.

Why We Need Dads

Once upon a time, there was a red-headed little princess, Gingerella, that lived in a two-story brick castle. She had a beautiful, white canopy bed, a brown pony named Christmas, and a three-story Barbie dream house. She had every toy imaginable and even had a playroom to share with her sister, who happened to also be her best friend. She had lots of clothes and plenty of room to play outside. This little girl had so many things, but there was a sense of something missing inside of her. She would play with her other friends at their houses, and, at bedtime, something magical would happen: their daddies would come home, eat dinner, and tell them good night. There was something inside of Gingerella that felt a sense of sadness and longing, but she wasn't sure just why.

Gingerella came from a home where the thought of the King made the Queen quite angry. The King was a four-letter word to the Queen, and she made certain that the entire kingdom knew it. And yet, Gingerella adored the King. It seemed that princesses should.

Gingerella would see the King on the weekends and for two weeks in the summer. There was a sense of identity that she missed not having the King there like her friends. She hated the way the King was talked about. It was confusing to her because she loved the Queen and the King. So, Gingerella learned to not talk about the King. She learned to push her feelings down to protect the King and herself. It changed Gingerella from a carefree princess to a caretaker and secret keeper. Princesses are not meant to bear the burdens of an entire castle on their backs.

We need dads. As girls, our dads are our first loves. If they tell us we are beautiful, we are. Smart, funny, or the best baseball player or ballerina that has ever been, then we are. How our dads see us influence how we see ourselves; even when we are grown, we have subtle whispers of that desire for approval from them. We so want to live up to who we want our dads to love. Why is it that girls and their dads' relationships are so vital and necessary to our self-esteem, security, and safety?

Have you ever been at the pool and watched a father play with his kids? A typical mom (or Mimi) has them coated in 150 SPF plus a swim shirt, a lifejacket, a sun-hat, swim shoes, and makes them wait thirty minutes after eating a cracker before they wade into the shallow end of the pool. But, the dad (or Paw Paw) slaps a sun shirt on a puddle jumper and sticks them on the sliding board. At the last minute, Paw Paw jumps in the pool, catches the child, who looks slightly terrified for a split second before squealing with laughter, and wants to do that for the rest of the afternoon. (This may be an actual story with our grandson. I can't imagine why our grandson loves Paw Paw to go on adventures with.)

Dads are the ones that throw the kids in the air and catch them while the moms pray silently and have 911 dialed on their phones, just waiting to hit "send." They are the adventurous ones and the tender ones too. From a young age, we need the safety of a man that loves us, just as we are. We need a hero, and we need to be loved, no matter what.

Dads have been given a pretty bad rap lately. A dad is so vital to a family. I heard a pastor say, "The best gift you can give your kids is to love their mom." I completely agree; love your wife well. I also think that, in this broken world that we live in, divorce happens; I came from it, and I was divorced. I think that the enemy has convinced many in our society that when a marriage or relationship ends, the kids' relationship with their dad ends as well. Unless it is an abusive relationship, I want to beg you to find a way to keep your children involved with their dad. It is so hard, but for their sake, find a counselor, pastor, family member, or very brave friend to help mediate a way to try and make it work.

And please, please, don't talk badly about your children's dad. Ladies, I feel like we do this sometimes in subtle ways. I mean, this can be while we are married. Trust me on this, every time you criticize your kid's dad, it's like taking fifty percent of them and saying, "Half of you is unworthy; half of you is bad." I understand what it is like to have strong feelings towards their dad, but they didn't choose him; *you did*. I know that sounds harsh, but as a woman that has been divorced, as well as a child of divorce, no one wins when harsh words are spoken. Hurtful words are so damaging to their hearts and self-esteem. I have seen kids that have been abused, living in foster care, that get violent when they hear someone talk badly about the parent that put them there. Broken relationships are a difficult thing for all of us. For the sake of your children, honor their parent, stay silent, and find a safe place *away from them* for you to talk.

Imagine, if you can, a world with no men. We have become a society where I am not even sure who is valued much anymore. I suppose it depends on who you are around, but one group that I see being valued less and less is the American man. For years now, men are made fun of on television and in the home. Man bashing could practically be an Olympic sport. Fewer men are staying married, getting married, and that means more kids without a dad in the home. God created man and then woman to be separate yet equal parts of a beautiful design. Why are we allowing the enemy to destroy what God created to bring life? Oh yeah, back to my imagination question, no men. No God-ordained, biblical marriages. No babies through natural conception. There are a whole lot of jobs that we as women would struggle with (this may not be a popular statement; actually, this paragraph is biblical and accurate, but not popular). We do not have the upper body strength that men do; we tend to have lower body strength. We need the unique wisdom that men have; they need the wisdom we have. We need men. Our society needs men, and I am so blessed to know some incredibly great ones. I know some really rotten ones too. I am choosing to let God redeem my memories of the bad and celebrate the gift of the good. Dads are men, and men are dads, and we need more and more great ones.

One of the biggest reasons that all these experiences matter is that how we see our dads tend to influence how we see God. Before you write that thought off, take a moment and think about how you see God when you feel like you failed. Do you see God as compassionate and loving? Distant and angry? Frustrated and disappointed? Judgmental and condemning? Absent? Does He see the best in you? Our underlying thoughts about

God, not what we tell people we think or we know to be true in scripture, can be quite similar to our experiences with our dads. You may be thinking, "What good does that information do for me, Courtnay? Now I feel discouraged; I can't go back and fix what negative things my dad did, and now it's impacting my relationship with God?"

The good news is that what we recognize can be addressed and changed. This is not meant to make anyone feel hopeless about their father because there is only one perfect father—God. That is *the first truth*: the only perfect father is God, and we can only learn who He is through the Bible, prayer, and time with Him.

The second truth is that our earthly fathers have traits that are not like our Heavenly Father. Our earthly father may get angry when we make mistakes; he may have abandoned us, he may lie to us, etc. This may make us feel like this is how God is. The only way to find out if our earthly father has traits like our Heavenly Father is through the first truth: get to know our Father in Heaven, and then we can recognize when we are giving our Heavenly Father a false identity. If we don't learn to recognize where we are giving God a false identity out of our own hurts, we are cheating ourselves out of His goodness. I have to identify the lies as lies and learn who God really is. No more false identities!

The third truth is that God has perfect attributes that we need. Write them down and study them so that, when the lies come, you have truths to combat them. A great example is this scripture in Numbers 23:19 (NIV): "God is not human, that he should lie, not a human being, that he should change his mind. Does he speak and then not act? Does he promise and not fulfill?"

We need dads. Maybe your story with your dad is a dysfunctional fairy tale, poor Gingerella. Many of us were blessed to have a dad that was present and wonderful. However, many of us didn't have one or wish the one we had could have just disappeared from existence. Many of us may have lost our dad through death or through his own choices. Maybe your dad was there in body, but not in mind. Whatever your story with the word dad is, if it brings you pain, my heart hurts for you. Sometimes we need to grieve childhood hurts in our adult bodies. We have just never given ourselves permission to do so. We have a Father that sounds so far away, but He is as close as a whisper. It is hard to believe that when you have hurt from the earthly man that should have loved you, and he should have, by the way. But God, He loves you, and He is the Father that you will always have if you accept Christ.

God loves you so much that He sent His Son for you and for all who will believe:

For God so loved the world that he gave his one and only Son, that whoever believes in him shall not perish but have eternal life.

John 3:16 (NIV)

This is how God showed his love among us: He sent his one and only Son into the world that we might live through him.

1 John 4:9 (NIV)

A father to the fatherless, a defender of widows, is God in his holy dwelling.

Psalm 68:5 (NIV)

Mothers, Daughters, and Twisters in the Trailer Park

There are a lot of complicated things here on planet Earth: quantum physics, chemistry, algebra and all things math, the inner workings of the solar system, meteorology, nuclear reactions. We have a better chance of understanding these things because someone on the planet has actually had some understanding of these things.

But mothers and daughters: these relationships are among the most wonderfully close and complex things that we have. Mothers are the ones we run to when we are hurt and who we call when we need advice. Moms are the ones that teach us how to be the women that we want to be; they are our role models and the ones we look up to. They can meet needs that no one else can.

Our mothers care for us, support us, and love us unconditionally unless, well, they don't. Then dear mercy filled heavens. We have two estrogen-filled, highly emotional, hurting women with a lot of history that collide. They need to get the junk out and resolve the hurts, if possible. Sometimes, the fight is over a turkey at Thanksgiving, and sometimes it is over a lifetime of abandonment and resentment. Our relationships are complicated, and our pain can run so deep.

The year 2020 was a challenging year for our nation. However, during the late hours of March 2 and early hours of March 3, things got even worse for the people of Tennessee. They were hit by a storm system that produced tornadoes ranging from category EF-0– EF-4. The twisters left a path of destruction across the Volunteer State, uprooting trees, structures, and lives indiscriminately.[3]

Much like those tornadoes, when we are hurting, we can tear through people's lives like a tornado through a trailer park. Trailers, or mobile homes, don't have the same foundations as traditionally built homes, so when a horrifically strong storm comes, they are just, well, gone. We can do the same thing when we are wounded. And the really awful part is that just like those tornados, it is indiscriminate. We don't address the deep wounds with our moms like we should. We take it out on others that we love. We attack the vulnerable and undeserving, those whose foundations were not expecting the storm. Are our children paying the price for the pain of our own childhoods? Or, are we taking our adult pain out on those that don't deserve it and rocking their firm foundations?

I pray this chapter doesn't apply to you, but I pray that you are brave enough to question if it does. I pray that you ask the Lord to examine your heart and see if you are the tornado, ripping through and tearing lives apart, or if you are the trailer, with your foundation shaken and torn to pieces. Some of us have been in the storm, and we haven't dealt with the pain. We don't even know how. We either fight constantly or avoid all confrontation. Some of us silently push every emotion down and let it stew like a horrific pressure cooker recipe, waiting to explode.

Some of us secretly hate shopping for Mother's Day cards and feel shameful for feeling the hate. We hate wishing we could buy the cards everyone else buys. Or we just wish our mother was different; we wish she kept our kids more, was cooler, understood us more, and was like our friend's moms. Or we wish we had the *Hallmark* movie mom that just took care of us, cooked for us, shopped for us, and never asked for anything in return. Or we wish she was still here, and we are upset that other women are constantly complaining about their mothers. We want to scream at the top of our lungs at every Mother's Day event that we attend with our friends, "All I want is my mom back!"

So, what is the remedy? There are no perfect mothers, not a single one. We as women need each other now more than ever. We need our moms, no matter how old we get. As we get older and our mothers die or are unable to be there for us physically, mentally, or emotionally, we can ask the Lord to bring women into our lives to love us. I do know that God works through people, and we were made for relationships. He has always provided the women that I have needed for the changing seasons of my life, but motherhood is one complicated gig.

We also have a responsibility to be there for other women in the changing seasons of their lives. Titus 2:3-4 (NIV) teaches us,

> Older women likewise are to be reverent in their behavior, not malicious gossips nor enslaved to much wine, teaching what is good, so that they may encourage the young women to love their husbands, to love their children.

Regardless of our age, we are called to mentor and help be spiritual mothers to each other. I promise, there is a woman in your life that needs your wisdom, guidance, and experience to help her mature in her walk with the Lord. These courageously needed acts of mentorship and loving our sisters in the faith can help fill in the gaps of the motherless around us or in us.

If you have hurt with your mom, I want to say, first and foremost, I am so sorry. Sometimes moms do the best they can, and it's not enough, and sometimes they don't try at all. Sometimes they leave physically when they didn't want to through death or through their own choices. Sometimes they leave mentally and abandon you with all of your hurt. I am making absolutely no excuses. I am acknowledging that your pain is so legitimate, even if you have never talked about it. I am grieving every Mother's Day church service with you where your heart races and you wish you could just disappear. I am hurting with you and hope you will give yourself permission to survey the trailer park of your heart and take time to grieve for what should have been and what you have lost.

Find a place to honor and love your mom. This can be a tough one when your heart has been "tornadoed." I heard someone say that sometimes the best thing your parents may have been capable of doing well was giving you life. Ask Jesus to help you work with that. Ask Jesus to help you with all of this. That is a great place to start and, if we can build from that as we heal, that is a blessing. What if the DNA that you share with her is all that you have to build on? What if every act that we do like

Christ is an act of love that reflects love back to them? For example, what if, when we have the opportunity to say the tornado response at a holiday get-together, we simply walk away as an act of respect? What if these simple changes in perspective could provide a huge blessing of promise from God, as taught in Exodus 20:12?

Just like a tornado, there are times we need help to dig out of the rubble. Seek help if you need to. If you have been fighting the same battle with your mom for years and years, or your wounds feel unforgivable, seek out a licensed Christian Counselor. Stop staying stuck. I talked about how we view our dads' impacts on how we see Father God. How we see our moms can impact our relationships with other women and how we parent our own children. That, my friends, is huge, and you can find healing from your wounds. We desperately need each other. We are commanded to mentor younger women, and we need to do that from a place of health, not trailer park destruction.

There is no way to prevent a tornado, but there is one sure way to clean up the wreckage that remains: the dispensing of love in heavy doses. See, 1 Corinthians 13:4-7 (NIV) teaches us that:

Love is patient, love is kind. It does not envy, it does not boast, it is not proud. It does not dishonor others, it is not self-seeking, it is not easily angered, it keeps no record of wrongs. Love does not delight in evil but rejoices with the truth. It always protects, always trusts, always hopes, always perseveres.

We all need to receive this kind of sincere, Godly love and need to practice giving it away as well.

Ladies, we have all caused damage and hurt people we love; we have been the tornadoes. We have been the trailers and had our foundations shaken or torn apart as well. Unfortunately, the storms of life will come. When they do, let's strive to show love and find love. Let's determine to search for Jesus in the remains.

You Are Going to Grieve Yourself to Death

We have many sayings here in the South: "You'll catch your death of a cold," "She was madder than a wet hen," "Bless her little heart," and the well-known "Kiss my grits." These are classics, and if you live here in the South, where I have been "born and raised" (another classic, I do believe), you will hear these on a regular basis used in their proper context. Let me give you a proper example of a good Southern conversation:

"David, did you see that lady give you the stink eye? You picked up the last pack of toilet paper, and she looked madder than a wet hen!"

"Baby, I didn't see she wanted it! Bless her heart."

This is how we use our Southernisms in everyday conversation. They are funny and make sense to us. There are a few that I have struggled with. A phrase I have heard said many times in my life as a Southern woman, but it may be a worldwide saying is, "Now pull it together. You are going to grieve yourself to death." And to be honest, the woman it was being said to wished to the good Lord above that she could. She wished the Lord would take her home so the pain would just end. Wouldn't it feel more merciful when the pain is so deep, and you don't know when you will feel anything close to normal again, to go be with the one you lost? I feel like this saying, "grieving yourself to death," is what we do about many other types of grief. When we hear the word grief, the first thing that comes to mind is death. Death leaves such a void and such an emptiness that we don't know if there will ever be a sense of normalcy again. There has been so much death, especially in 2020. We have not been allowed to grieve as we should; we have not been able to even lose our normal, normally! We have not had funerals as we should, church as we should, or physical touch as we should, just to name a few, and we need all of it to get through death and loss.

When I found out from many specialists that I could not have another child after my daughter, my world shattered into a million fragile pieces. I was still young because I was young when I had her. So, I was told so many hurtful things by helpful people. I was told to be thankful for her. I was told it was a blessing, "I mean, who would even want to bring another child into this world with things being so crazy." Well, after fertility drugs and surgeries, I got pregnant again. Everyone rejoiced! Then I lost the baby. People told me that God allows these things for a reason. I was young. I would probably get pregnant again. And I did. And I lost it, again. And I got pregnant for the third time after my daughter and lost that baby as well. I felt so incredibly alone and misunderstood. I wanted my babies, and I wanted my pain to be acknowledged. I wanted their short lives to be acknowledged. And for all that was good in the world, I wanted someone to say something that wasn't so stupid and hurtful to my wounded heart!

Pain and grief and all the awfulness that is encompassed within them are often ignored. Many times, we tend to say something so wrong instead of simply acknowledging that we have no clue what the person is going through. A simple "I am so sorry" or "I am praying for you" and then actually praying for the grieving person or people is enough when we don't know what to do or say. It is something that comes up a lot when counseling with clients: the wounds people had on top of their grief because people said really hurtful things. Being present and showing compassion in silence is better than saying things because we don't know what to say.

There has been so much loss and so much awfulness, but grief and hurt come in many cruel packages.

We can grieve and hurt over the end of the lives of those we love, the end of relationships, friendships, or dreams and plans. It is all just so incredibly painful.

Relationship grief doesn't get acknowledged like it should. When a relationship dies, a part of us can as well. And we don't acknowledge it fully within ourselves and the damage that it does inside of us. We don't acknowledge it with those that we love and realize that the pain can wound us and leave us with scars. Unchecked and unhealed, relational grief can leave us with trust issues and change how we view other people in the future. We tend to think of this as male and female relationships, but what about our friendships? Sometimes losing our friendships can be like losing a family member. What about when a girlfriend deceives or betrays us? In this age of "social media must be the truth," are you being destroyed publicly? Do we grieve the wounds like we should, or are we still hurting over them years later? We can harbor unforgiveness and bitterness, and that can hinder our relationship with God and others. We drag our heavy baggage into our next relationship, and the next person pays for the sins of another. And that's not right. And we all lose, and we all grieve more.

What about the grief of when our dreams die? The year 2020, and possibly the years to follow, have really marked that reality as individuals and as a nation. People had planned weddings, trips to mark significant occasions, graduation ceremonies, parties to celebrate anniversaries, holiday gatherings, and other life-defining moments. They were deleted from our lives like a dry eraser on the whiteboard of our life plans. Just like grief, the messages and the reasons why were confusing and caused strife among loved ones as to why things had to change. One of the many things about grief that is so hard is that the loss is something that can't be regained. We don't know if the people we wanted to attend those events will be available or if it could be the same. Time keeps passing, we keep hurting, and life feels forever changed. And life is forever changed, and we can't control it, and we don't like it.

Imagine a beautiful hot air balloon, full and ready to take flight. After all, it takes something as large and majestic as a hot air balloon to contain something like a lifetime full of dreams. This particular balloon is so special; it contains our expectations, hopes, and wishes for the future. We aren't even aware that over the course of our entire life, we are putting our future hopes and dreams in there, and yet, it contains so many beautiful things. We attend our cousin's wedding, and we think about what kind of cake we may have and what song would be our first dance one day. We go to a friend's graduation, we see their funny hat and all their friends, and we think that one day we will have that experience. We continue to live our lives and put all of those normal events in our hot air balloon, just waiting for the day for the fire to light the torch and cause it to take flight. We assume we will jump in that basket. We assume we have a balloon. Everyone has a balloon, right? Grief feels like a big ugly thief that comes along and shreds our balloon and extinguishes our torch. It just never occurred to us that there would be no balloons or that we would have to reinvent them. Our dreams have been our culture and our normal. It is normal and healthy to grieve the loss of those dreams.

You can fill in the blank with your own grief experience. The point is that it can be so many different things. Grief is loss that hurts your soul and changes your life. Grief changes your path and changes you. Change doesn't mean it defines you or makes you worse.

One of my dearest friends told me her cancer was a gift. She was in the process of grieving more losses than I could fathom, but as the disease changed her, it forced her to look at her life in a different way. She let go of things that she needed to be let go of. She held on to things that she treasured tighter. Change doesn't mean bad. In the hands of Jesus, He can make the difficult places something better than we can ever imagine.

I have walked the path of grief more times than I would have ever thought possible. I have also walked the path of grief with many others. All of us that grieve have some questions in common: am I even allowed to grieve this pain, this long, this way? Am I going to survive? Will I ever have "normal" again?

Have you ever seen the show *Hoarders*? It is a show that examines the lives of people that have held on to so many items that they cannot move through their homes, literally. Every newspaper, soup can, and container has so much emotion attached to it that it has to stay. It has to remain to the degree that they have risked their health, their safety, and the ability to remain in the home they love safely. The show comes in when they are at the point of being evicted, and the house is sometimes being condemned. Those items started out as needed, necessary, and useful for a time, and then they became harmful. And ugly. And now those things keep people away. People don't want to come near, and they don't understand, so they stay far away when what the person with all the stuff that holds them captive needs is love. This is how our choices with our grief can become. We can choose what we do with the awfulness of what we have.

I want you to understand that we all have free will and the ability to choose what to do with all of our overwhelming pain. Pain is ugly and necessary for a time. We have to feel it to process the loss and allow Jesus to come in and heal our broken places. Many of us have come to know Jesus in a deeper way through pain and grief. Some of our best friends come to us through shared experiences and loss.

First, it takes time. That is the thing none of us wants to hear. We don't get over our losses overnight. It takes as long as it takes for you, and that is not the same as someone else. We have to process what we have in front of us. We have to feel the emotions, not run from them. What emotions should we feel? The ones you feel. Everyone is different, and everyone feels different things and may even feel all the different emotions at different times.

Secondly, cry until there are no tears left to cry. Or, get angry and get a cheap plastic bat and take it out on a big, safe tree. Or get whatever emotion you are feeling about your losses and feel them in a safe and healthy way. Feel all of the feels. Understand that they will probably come back, and they may come back when you don't expect them. Get help when you need to from a counselor or a friend that can be trusted.

Next, consider journaling your pain. Write out everything you are feeling. It feels terrible to write and cry about all the awful things you are experiencing. It is also amazing to read years later and see how far God has brought you or to be able to share it with someone who needs the encouragement that you did make it.

And when you have done all of this or, better yet, made it through all of this, invite God to heal your shattered heart. The Lord tells us in Psalm 147:3 (NIV), "He heals the brokenhearted and binds up their wounds." God is true to His promises. He will heal what you invite Him to heal. No fancy words or eloquent prayers; just the name of Jesus and a sincere request are all you need.

Asking God to bind up your wounds is like having the most critical condition in the world with a very small chance of survival. There is only one physician on the planet that can heal you, and He wants to take your case. Why would you refuse that care, that healing power? God has a 100 percent success rate, and He is ready to help you.

We have a lot of sayings in the South, that is true. But they are just things we say. Please, don't "grieve yourself to death." Jesus and the Word of God are all truth, and He promises comfort, hope, and eternal life to all who believe in Him. No saying in the North, South, East, or West will be able to offer you that.

In Defense of Our Parents

I remember I was five years old when my mom and dad separated for good. My mom sat my sister and me down on our orange corduroy couch and told us he was leaving and not coming back. From the best of my recollection, my first question was, "Can we go to Bam-Baw's now?" It may have been an unreasonable question for a twenty-year-old, but it was a completely logical one for a five-year-old. Bam-Baw was our eighty-pound grandmother that was also somehow ten feet tall and completely bulletproof, had no money, and yet lived in an ivory castle. She was all things good and safe. Every single one of her grandchildren, as different as we are, has this same opinion of Bam-Baw.

My dad traveled five days a week, so it wasn't that earth-shattering to me that he wasn't coming back. I mean, I was five. I was five, but I was expected to be twenty. This pattern of being everything to everyone, being the strong woman to the hurting, taking care of those that could not, or more accurately, would not take care of themselves, defined me. At the ripe old age of five, it began.

My mom was so upset at my lack of being upset that she loaded us up in her super cool, wood-paneled station wagon. That thing was so big that my brother used to hide in the very back seat. It folded down and then opened up to face directly at oncoming traffic through its giant, oversized pane of glass. My brother used to hide in it and then pop up and scare my mother when she was driving. Yep, growing up in the seventies was truly a constant game of playing chicken with death.

Anyway, my mom finally took us to our grandmother's house. I began to learn something from a very young age that most of us do not realize we know: *we adapt our behaviors and emotions to please those we are most concerned about.* Our concerns can manifest themselves as worry, fear, anxiety, or a simple desire to please those we love, but we are willing to adapt and comfort them to get them through difficult times. If it's temporary, that is empathy, that is healthy, and that is good. But if it becomes our identity, it can become exhausting, and for those of us with sensitive souls, this takes a serious toll on us in every way.

My parent's marriage ended. The effects of their divorce lasted my entire childhood and into my adolescent years. My siblings and I became pawns in a chess game that had no winners. There would be no kindness between my parents again—no sitcom, brief moments of well wishes.

The nastiness of their divorce took a toll on me that I did not fully realize until my early twenties. I just wanted peace. I had become the most well-conditioned, highly-skilled wartime negotiator in world history. If it was possible for oil and water to come into agreement and somehow mix, by golly, I was willing to try and sit down and make it happen.

The divorce also impacted my identity in positive and negative ways. On the negative side, I worry about people and situations that I really should not worry about. I just want everyone happy, like everyone. This desire can make me miserable because I can't control that! I love to give, and take care of, and listen, and nurture you, but I do not like the idea of needing to be taken care of. That need makes me feel vulnerable and needy, and I don't like vulnerability. It can feel like weakness to me. Conflict makes me nervous; I need to run if the conflict doesn't lead to resolution. To fight and fight and fight with no end is so pointless, and I can run faster than a jaguar with a case of energy drinks in its system. This can make deep relationships really hard for me because relationships do have conflict. These negative attributes: worrying, risking vulnerability, and avoiding conflict are things I continue to ask the Lord to help me work through.

On the positive side, I want to be fought for. I want to be ferociously pursued if you love me. Do you know why? Because I will fight for you. I have been called the "golden retriever of friends." I purposely have a small group of really close friends. I want to love them well, and I can't do that with a large group of people. I will stay by their side, no matter what, because I am loyal. If the friendship ends, every secret they ever shared, every story they ever told, goes to my grave with me because I am trustworthy. These qualities: pursuing those you care for, loyalty, and being trustworthy matter a lot to me.

The negatives of my parents' divorce are not excuses for who I am or things that I cannot work to change. I have learned to recognize that my parents' hurt-filled divorce did help define me. But let's be really honest here. I have never asked, but I am certain that my parents did not sit down in a room and say, "How can we use our failed marriage to mess our kids up as much as possible?" And yet, that is how we treat many of our parents today. We look at our parents' areas of failure and think they took a rifle, filled it full of wide-sweeping buckshot, and aimed it directly at us. If your parent or parents have destroyed you, my heart truly breaks. My parents did a lot of damage to my heart, and now my mom is gone. The chance for any conversations that could bring healing on this side of heaven is gone for me, so I truly understand your pain more than I am willing to share in this book. But what I am saying is: for the vast majority of parents, the pain that has been inflicted upon us was an over-spilling of the pain that was swelling up inside of them.

When we bought our new home, I had a gas cooktop for the first time. I was cooking and went to get ready and left the kitchen for a while. As I started to walk back, I got really dizzy and felt weird. When I reached the cooktop, I was confused. The dial was on, but the fire was out. I hadn't turned anything off. I kept feeling woozy. I believe it was the Lord that made me realize the liquid in my pot boiled over, extinguished the flame, but not the gas. That gas was coming out just as quickly as ever. It was just doing what gas does. That gas was providing heat when there was a flame, but in the absence of a heat source, it can become toxic. Such a thing also happens to the pain that is not dealt with inside of our souls.

I was in my twenties when I realized my parents were adults doing the best they could as people that happened to be my parents. It hit me like one of those anvils being dropped off a cliff from a cartoon. I was trying to make a marriage work, take care of a child, enduring my second miscarriage, and working a very demanding job, and I snapped. Not on a person, but in the privacy of my own car. I was in management and worked about fifty hours that week. I still needed to go home, do homework, dinner, and laundry, and I thought about how this adulting thing was more than I could really handle. And then there was the loss of another baby. It was just too much. I remembered pulling my car into a parking lot, and I cried and cried and cried until there was no liquid left in my body. I really thought about running away to Zimbabwe or some land where I could just start all over, never to be heard from again. See, my pot boiled over, shut off the flame, and all I could feel was the toxic effects of the gas in my life. In that moment, I thought about all that my parents were and were not, and they became people and not just my parents. When that happened, I was ready to start a path towards forgiveness.

Forgiveness is a funny thing. It's not a double-edged sword; it's more like a dagger with many sides and a velvet handle. God commands us to forgive. Matthew 6:14 (NIV) says, "For if you forgive other people when they sin against you, your heavenly Father will also forgive you." I need His forgiveness, so I have to forgive others. The issue of forgiveness and the pain that necessitates forgiveness brings a lot of people to counseling. I was one of those people many years ago that needed counseling for many deep wounds that I continue to work through to this day. The challenge with forgiveness is that it is hard and complex. Many times, the people that wounded you are not even sorry or aware of what they did. Some may not be healthy enough to deal with their own damage or still be alive to work through the issues with you. Many people feel like forgiveness means reconciliation. That is not always possible or even healthy. You may be thinking, "Courtnay, that doesn't sound very Christ-like." And yet, Romans 12:18 (NIV) teaches us, "If it is possible, as far as it depends on you, live at peace with everyone." The words *if it is possible* and *as far as it depends on you* should help set someone free. Someone reading this has forgiven someone but trying to have a relationship with them is like trying to make a bobcat act like a domesticated housecat dressed in a Christmas sweater; *impossible.* Be set free, friend. *Peace is not possible with everyone because we all have free will, and not all people want peace.*

Forgiveness can be a daily decision. You pray for the strength to forgive what your mind struggles to forget. You choose to make a decision, and, eventually, your emotions follow. You pray for empathy. You ask God to help you see them through His eyes; that wrecked me and changed everything.

The reason forgiveness is like a dagger with many sides is that you will be required to forgive your parents. You can have the perfect parents or the most awful parents in the universe. They are all human, and they will all make mistakes. They all need grace. We all need grace. They will require a lot of different types of forgiveness. Sometimes, yours may ask for forgiveness; sometimes, yours won't. Forgive them anyway and do it for you and do it because you have to have it from the God that forgave you.

You will need to forgive yourself. You will grow up and wish you were a better adult child. You will wish you had asked more questions, tried a little harder, lingered a little longer. You will wish you knew more. Forgive yourself. You need that velvet handle to be brave enough to take it in your hands and have the gentle courage that it takes to forgive. That was made by God to refine you into something wonderful and beautiful and to use your testimony to help others work through their pain.

Your parents, whomever they may be, made you. They may have given you to your adoptive parents; they gave you life. They may have been broken and absent and empty and wounded. They may have been so abusive that you have never spoken of the atrocities you have seen and the fear you have grown up in. They may have been the epitome of perfection, attending every ballgame and working every bake sale. They may have fallen somewhere in the middle of all of these scenarios or nowhere on this page. But your parents, whoever they may be, made you. And the world is thankful for that.

I Think My Eyeballs Are Stuck to My Pillow and Other Grief-Related Problems

There is something quite ironic about being married to an eye doctor when you have cried your eyes out. I thought that was just one of those sayings. Then one day, after months of heartbreak all around me, I woke up, and those little rascals were lying right there on the pillow next to my head. I mean, I think so; I couldn't actually see them because I just mentioned that I had cried them right out of my head. My husband, Dr. J. David Aycock, denies the medical validity of this story, but I do feel like that is what should have happened.

I am just so tired of crying. And I really am trying to hold it together, but I see beautiful women of all different ages and shades and races and stories and experiences being torn apart. My heart breaks at their stories, and their tears become my own. We are indeed the body of Christ, and we share each other's pain.

Death is just so final here on earth. And I am tired of death. There just are not enough tears in our bodies to pour out when we don't bring a loved one home. Home with us is where they belong, right? But when then the hearse comes, the friends leave, the casseroles are gone, and that giant void is not just a hole in the ground; what are we supposed to do? Aren't we tired of hearing, "I'm sorry for your loss," and yet, what else are people supposed to say? We go through times where we are angry at what people say, and we are angry at what people don't say. It all just hurts, and we need it to stop. I cry for the separation of loved ones here on earth.

What about the ending of a marriage? A woman once said something to me, going through a horribly nasty divorce that she didn't want, that I have never forgotten. She told me his death would be easier than the divorce. She could grieve, hurt, and find closure. But the divorce was awful, and she thought it was killing her from the inside out. She wasn't wishing he would die; there was just no foreseeable end to her pain. She still had to see him with their children; she still had to communicate with him about old finances, which brought up old pain, old feelings, old misery, and new grief, over and over and over again. I cry for her pain, which feels greater than death, for a love that is one-sided now.

Divorce is so incredibly hard. Two people are torn apart by one person that promised to always be there but has chosen not to be anymore, or two people have agreed not to remain married to each other. It seems, sometimes, that we have forgotten that marriage wasn't always just a cultural concept; it was a *covenant made to God*. Marriage and the shrapnel it leaves behind when it ends isn't discussed because it has become culturally acceptable to let it die. I have made the decision to divorce before. It is not a decision that is as easy as the culture makes it sound. "Normal" does not equal consequence-free. Just because it has become more normal does not minimalize the pain of millions of husbands, wives, and children that lost a two-parent home. A death occurs on a divorce day; the dreams and plans of those men and women have now died. The dreams may be over, and court papers may be signed, but the new pain is very, very real. This is hard, and the pain of this loss may be rarely discussed, but it is often felt and very real. I cry for the loss of their hopes and plans.

Women are blown to shreds when cancer comes, and parts of their bodies begin to disappear, never to return again. Women and the toll that cancer takes is an elite club that absolutely no one wants to join. Women are strong, brave, and remarkable. Women's hearts can simultaneously carry weakness and tender pain that they will share with other women fighting the same fight. I cannot believe the love, support, and kindness that we see in women fighting cancer, the awful and the holy coexisting. And, this makes me cry for the goodness of God, walking with those whose lives are falling apart.

I have someone in my life that has made hurting me feel like a hobby and a sport. I have sought professional help and much wise counsel. People who love me and know me and the situation well have advised me it's time to stop allowing myself to be abused for the millionth time. The pain of realizing you have spent a lifetime being used with no gratitude or real love is more than gut-wrenching. I pray the relationship can be something it has never been, but it takes two healthy people for tango to happen. Otherwise, you have one healthy person dancing twice as hard, fooling themselves into believing that the dance is working. It's a gut-wrenching thing to come to grips with the fact that it is not. I cry for what has not been and for what may never be.

I am tired of crying. So are many of you. I wish I could come to see you and we could weep together. We would ugly cry for as long as it takes for one-tenth of 1 percent of your load to feel lighter. We would go through boxes of tissues and eat tons of carbs or carrots or whatever it takes until we found some comfort.

What do we do when tears are not enough? What do we do when we just can't cry enough? What do we do when we keep looking for comfort, but we cannot find any? It feels like God has forsaken us, but I can assure you of this, the God of the universe is greater than anything we ever feel. *The God of the universe is greater than anything we ever feel.* We can feel forsaken, but God will always stay, and our crying will end.

Our Father did tell us in Psalm 30:5 (MSG): "The nights of crying your eyes out give ways to days of laughter."

We all hate grief, loss, weeping, and tears. I gave a few scenarios, but I could fill this book with the pain of what I have hurt over or my loved ones and clients have shared. So what do we do when we have no more tears to cry? Many of us distract ourselves with busyness. The world offers many things to get our attention focused on. Our flesh really wants to go around the pain; God wants us to go through it. You may be thinking, why? That is cruel and mean and could not possibly serve any purpose other than cause even more pain.

I remember reading this verse. It has become a foundation that I cling to in times of pain and is even one of the foundational verses of our ministry, Desert Streams.

Second Corinthians 1:3-4 (NIV) teaches us a truth about pain that can help us to see a purpose:

Praise be to the God and Father of our Lord Jesus Christ, the Father of compassion and the God of all comfort, who comforts us in all our troubles, so that we can comfort those in any trouble with the comfort we ourselves receive from God.

When we understand that God will comfort us because that is who He is, the Father of compassion and God of all comfort, it helps me understand that if I have a relationship with Him, as I go through the pain with Him, He will take care of me. As I go through it with Him: death, divorce, cancer, and other unspeakable pain, He will comfort me so I can comfort other people with what He gives me. That allows me to see a glimmer of hope and purpose in my misery.

So, there is a redemptive purpose to my tears: tears can be cleansing and healing. There are actually things we need to cry about. Tears can be unifying. Someone else may need you to cry with them over your shared pain. Tears can be what you haven't shed that may be what could help you move forward and release your hurts, fears, and anger.

I want to put your minds and eyes at ease. I have actually confirmed it is safe to cry as much as you need to. God designed those eyeballs to hang on through all those tears.

The Story That Didn't End

This is the chapter I didn't want to write. This was the chapter I never, ever planned to write. This is the one I did not want to share because so few people know this part of my life. I have prayed and asked God that if it could save one life or change one mind, my pain has been worth it. So, here I go.

I remember going to the drug store on Sunset Drive when I was eighteen years old. I had no money, but the pharmacist had extended a small line of credit to me (the perk of being a small-town girl). I remember taking my daughter in and buying a bottle of sleeping pills and sliding a few more items into the purchase so they would hopefully go unnoticed. I didn't know if there was anything more pathetic than having to charge a bottle of pills that would never be paid for because I couldn't think of anyone to pay the bill. I went home to my apartment, put her to bed that evening, and opened that bottle. The wrestling with God began. I wanted to die. I felt alone and completely overwhelmed. My plans were gone. My daughter cried constantly, and I didn't feel that even she loved me. I had given up everything to raise her. I was working two jobs to support her, all alone. My boyfriend and I had just broken up.

I had chosen life, but I felt that life had chosen to forsake me.

I heard her cry. The Lord began to remind me that He has always sustained me through a life that has been hard. He has always provided, but it has not been easy. And if I chose to take my life, who would raise my daughter?

I may have chosen to save her life, but two years later, she saved mine.

Hopelessness is so powerful when it gets a hold of your heart and mind that it feels like the only option. I understand why suicide has climbed in the last few years. I want to tell whoever is reading this: please, do not do something permanent that can't be undone. I have walked the devastating path of pain with too many family members that lost a loved one with nothing left but questions. I thank God I didn't go through with my plan, especially now that I see all that the Lord has redeemed out of my brokenness.

I would never have thought that, thirty years later, I would be wrestling the demon of suicide once again.

My health struggles had been ongoing and frustrating. We had been trying to get answers from any avenue you can imagine. Just like so many women, we struggle, but we push through because people around us need us. We suffer in silence. Over the course of my life, I have had various surgeries, and I recovered. I limped through life, but I moved. We knew we would eventually get to the root cause—well, David believed we would get to the root, and I would be fully back to normal. I felt like I may find out what was really wrong with me while standing next to Jesus, looking down at my own autopsy. After close to a decade of suffering, let's just say, my hope was getting depleted. It was the perfect setup for what was coming.

In November of 2018, I started having serious balance issues. I broke a piece of furniture when I fell. Then came the pain in my head. I don't mean I had a headache, I mean I thought my head had exploded, and an icepick was sticking out of my eye. I couldn't tolerate light or sounds. I was so nauseated I couldn't handle food. Being still hurt and moving hurt. I saw a neurologist that was so kind that he was giving me samples and trying experimental things. He saw me twice a week. After three weeks, he said, "Mrs. Aycock, I don't know what is wrong with you. I think you need to go to a pain clinic until we can get you in with someone else." I worked in addiction and knew I wasn't willing to go

down the pain clinic road. And the "someone else" was a
six-month wait. I was in such misery that I didn't sleep.
I would get up at 2 a.m. every morning, stumble to my
chair in the living room, quietly play praise music, and
beg Jesus to just take me home and send David a good
wife. He needed a wife that wasn't so broken. He needed
a wife that didn't feel like her tears were acid pouring
from her eyes. He needed a wife that was fixable. I knew
I was not fixable anymore.

This was my life for several months. Months. Every
single hour of every single day. I cried, I prayed, I wor-
shipped. I didn't share how deep my despair was except
with a few of my closest people. Thank God they are
mighty, mighty warriors in the faith. They fasted. They
prayed. David fasted. He prayed. They were all fighting
hell for me.

The enemy came for my life again, but he wanted me
to do it by my own hands again. He told me how I was a
burden to David. He told me if people really knew how
sick I was, they wouldn't care. He told me I would suffer
like this forever. He told me I would never feel better.
He told me death was so much better. I listened to him.
And then...

The Spirit of God that lives in me awakened me. I
got up and took the things he was tempting me to take
my life with and locked them up in my car. I laid on the
floor of my kitchen and determined in my heart to tell

it all to David the moment that he got home—the lies, the temptation, the fears, all of it. See, darkness dispels when light is exposed to it. It was emotionally and spiritually the turning point for my health journey. I have not wrestled with those suicidal feelings again.

So what saved my life?

Accountability. You cannot exist in solitude, especially when you are struggling and in the depths of despair. The Word reminds us in Galatians 6:2 (NIV) to "Carry each other's burdens, and in this way you will fulfill the law of Christ."

Getting help. If you are entertaining thoughts of suicide or ongoing hopelessness, talk to someone. It is difficult when you feel hopeless, but please, for the sake of the future of those around you, talk to your doctor, pastor, or contact a counselor. There is so much help available to you. If you are contemplating suicide right now, call 911 or go to the closest emergency room. Remember, God works through people. Cry out to Him as you seek help. Hebrews 4:16 (NIV): "Let us then approach God's throne of grace with confidence, so that we may receive mercy and find grace to help us in our time of need."

Daily time with God. Even in my darkest, darkest days, I played scripture quietly on my phone. I kept worship music on. I refused to believe the lie that God was doing this to me. He has been too good to me all of my life. He will use this for good. I pray He will use this to encourage one person. If my story, my pain, saves one life, it is not wasted pain. He has used it to change me. I am a more mature woman of God. I know what matters, and I release what doesn't matter a lot easier. I don't have the ability to do this life and fight these battles without Him. And I cling to this truth: "I remain confident of this: I will see the goodness of the Lord in the land of the living" (Psalm 27:13, NIV).

I awaited an appointment with a neurologist that specialized in headaches. She was an answer from God Himself. I am still struggling, and more things have happened since this started, but I have also written this book in the middle of this. Our ministry is seven years old and continues to grow. Our marriage is stronger and more beautiful, and I know how deeply and unconditionally I am loved. The amazing thing about being a believer and a Christ-follower is that most of your life will not make sense. You will see the hard and the suffering and the beauty and the blessings and stand in awe. You will be speechless. Beauty from ashes.

But God.

About the Author

Courtnay Aycock was born, raised, and made it all the way back to Monroe, NC. She graduated from Wingate University with her bachelor's degree and completed her master's program at Liberty University. Courtnay is board certified as a pastoral counselor through the American Association of Christian Counselors. She has worked as a pastoral counselor, writer, and teacher, helping countless women and families through her and her husband's non-profit organization, Desert Streams Ministry. She enjoys time with her children, her grandson, Parker, family, and friends when not working. And she believes, if she were not so busy, she could find a hobby. Her husband, however, doesn't really buy that theory.

BIBLICAL SOLUTIONS TO LIFE'S PROBLEMS

Courtnay Aycock is the co-founder of Desert Streams Ministry. It was founded in 2014 with a mission to provide biblical guidance, teaching, and support to those in need through the power of Jesus Christ. Desert Streams has existed by donations and has helped countless people through individual counseling. As we are turning the page on a new chapter, we are now focused on groups and conferences in order to reach and help more people at a time. Our mission stays the same—helping people through the power of Jesus Christ.

If you would like to know more about our ministry or would be interested in having Courtnay teach or speak at your church or event, please visit our website: dsministry.com.

Watch our weekly devotionals on Facebook: *www.facebook.com/desertstreamsministry/.*

Endnotes

1 "The Love Boat," Wikimedia Foundation, accessed May 23, 2021, https://en.wikipedia.org/w/index.php?title=The_Love_Boat&oldid=1034554804.
2 The Facts of Life (TV series)," Wikimedia Foundation, accessed July 24, 2021, https://en.wikipedia.org/w/index.php?title=The_Facts_of_Life_(TV_series)&oldid=1030817226.
3 "TN Twister – Stories of What the Tornado Didn't Destroy," Justin Harvey and Metro Arts Nashville THRIVE Grant, accessed 24 Mar. 2021, tntwister.com.